THE HUMOROUS MUSINGS OF A SCHOOL PRINCIPAL

By
Paul A. McClure

OLD PRINCIPALS NEVER DIE

OR

WHAT IS A TEACHER?

Walk sober off before the sprightlier age
Comes tittering on, and shoves you off the stage.

Alexander Pope

The Humorous Musings of a School Principal

Published by

The Lincoln-Herndon Press, Inc.
818 South Dirksen Parkway
Springfield, Illinois 62703
(217) 522-2732

Printed in the United States of America.

Library of Congress Cataloguing-in-Publication Data

ISBN 0-942936-32-9
Library of Congress Catalogue Card Number 97-074592
First Printing

Typography by Spiro Affordable Graphic Services

WHAT IS A TEACHER?

A TEACHER IS:

A PROPHET   The teacher knows the day the principal will visit his or her class.

AN INTERPRETER   The teacher re-writes all school directives in understandable English.

A CITIZEN   The teacher votes whenever a school levy is on the ballot.

A BELIEVER   The teacher believes the school board will grant a 10% salary increase.

A FRIEND   The teacher is a friend of the person next door because they have common enemies.

A PLANNER	The teacher plans all illnesses to take place on Fridays and Mondays.
A CULTURAL BUILDER	The teacher knows the difference between B.O. and the smell of marijuana.

Central Office Axiom: Increased paperwork at the central office requires more employees, which in turn requires more space to house the added employees, which in turn produces more paperwork, which in turn increases the need for more employees, which in turn...

Education, like living, happens one day at a time.

90-10 Law: Superintendents and their assistants spend 90% of their time dealing with the routine projects and only 10% on the important ones.

Every school system has at least one phantom teacher — one who only pretends to teach.

All teachers should be disliked by at least one student.

THE EYE'S HAVE IT

YOU WOULDN'T BELIEVE ME WHEN I TOLD YOU SHE HAD EYES IN BACK OF HER HEAD.

Ambiguity, whatever it is, teachers must learn to live with it.

Blessed are superintendents who are constantly changing things, for they shall make many enemies.

MAYBE HE HAD BETTER BEGIN LOOKING
FOR A NEW JOB

YOU SAY YOU HAVE THESE RECURRING DREAMS THAT THE THREE TEACHERS YOU FIRED ARE THE NEW MEMBERS OF THE SCHOOL BOARD?

The difference between experienced superintendents and inexperienced ones, in addition to salary, is: the experienced superintendents recognize their mistakes and can repeat them.

Isn't it surprising all the nice things the principal says about a teacher at the retirement party that were never mentioned during the yearly evaluation?

AT LEAST THE TEAM HAD FUN

WE DIDN'T WIN ANY SWIMMING MEETS THIS YEAR, BUT WE DID HAVE A MIRACULOUS SEASON. NO ONE DROWNED!

When school boards receive an unexpected tax windfall, expenses equaling the amount of the windfall immediately show up.

Teachers—when you call in sick, the principal seldom believes you.

It's a sign of aging when a father notices how young his son's teachers look.

BEAUTY IS IN THE EYES OF THE BEHOLDER

THE DESCRIPTION OF HIS TEACHER AS GIVEN BY SON TO HIS FATHER

THE PERSON HIS FATHER MET AT THE FIRST PTA MEETING

In many of our school systems a majority of the teachers are worth more than they are paid and a few are paid more than they are worth.

A teacher is a pessimist who thinks every teacher has the same personality he or she has.

On snow days, the main question is not "Will we have school today?" but, "Will we be able to play the football game tonight?"

Why can't ineffective teachers fall out of teaching as easily as they fell in?

One description of teachers' lesson plans—pieces of fiction.

September is the happiest month of the year for parents of school age students.

When a problem child enrolls in a school he or she will be assigned to the teacher with the largest class.

"NO FIGHTS, NO SPITBALLS, NO ONE TALKING, EVERYBODY DOING THEIR SCHOOLWORK, I MUST BE IN HEAVEN."

Old teachers never die. They can't afford it.

Much of a superintendent's success is more by luck than by merit.

College personnel often become so far removed from the classroom that they do not understand the real problems teachers face.

Any educational theory can be supported by facts providing the person expounding the theory gathers them.

If teachers of 50 years ago were suddenly resurrected, only June, July and August would be the same.

Absurdity is when a beginning teacher attempts to buy and pay for a new car without first visiting the credit union.

MAYBE HE'S JUST A CHIP OFF THE OLD BLOCK!

IF YOU FIND OUT HOW TO KEEP JOHNNY'S MIND OFF GIRLS, LET ME KNOW. HIS FATHER HAS THE SAME PROBLEM.

Superintendent addressing parents during the first open house of a new school: "We built this fine building squabble by squabble."

Give a minor problem to a school psychologist and it will quickly become a major one.

The chief difference between a clean desk and a cluttered one is: in a clean desk all the junk is carefully stashed in the drawers.

Some school systems believe that teachers should be seen and not heard, especially at negotiations time.

Isn't it amazing how teachers spend four years preparing to teach, but immediately forget everything they learned on that first day in the classroom?

The higher the level of incompetence among administrators, the more assistants needed.

I once had a student who kept a notebook titled "Handbook of Useless Information." I often wondered, did he eventually become an author of an education text?

THIS LETTER IS FROM THE LOCAL TEACHER'S UNION. SHALL WE PLAY ALONG WITH THEM FOR A COUPLE OF WEEKS BEFORE WE OFFER THEM A 1% INCREASE OR SHOULD WE SAVE TIME AND DO IT NOW?

In some school districts at negotiations time, the teachers ask the school board for a 10% raise, speak out loudly for 6%, and then accept whatever the board offers them.

Wouldn't it be a bitch at negotiations time if both sides were agreeable?

Law of intelligence for coaches of a girls seventh grade basketball teams: They have to be just smart enough to understand the game, but dumb enough to think it is important.

7th GRADE GIRL'S BASKETBALL GAMES DON'T LAST FOREVER. IT ONLY SEEMS THAT WAY.

THE PRINCIPAL ASKED ME TO COACH THE GIRL'S SEVENTH GRADE BASKETBALL TEAM THIS YEAR.

When two or more educators get together, they usually will find something to gripe about.

AT LEAST HE'S NOT CARRYING A BALL BAT.

JOHN, THAT NEW TEACHER IN ROOM 202 HAS GOOD DISCIPLINE, BUT DON'T YOU THINK HE IS GOING A LITTLE TOO FAR TELLING THE KIDS HE HAS A BLACK BELT IN KARATE?

Advice to teachers: If at first you don't succeed, try reading the teacher's manual.

Many history teachers go to their graves never knowing for certain the number of years in four score and seven.

HE KNOWS HE'S AN OLD-TIMER

ARE YOU TELLING ME YOUR HISTORY BOOK ONLY
DEVOTES TWO PAGES TO WORLD WAR II? WHY, I SPENT
TWO YEARS IN THOSE MOSQUITO-INFESTED JUNGLES.
I'M SURPRISED THEY HAVE THE DATES RIGHT.

ANYBODY CAN REWRITE HISTORY

IT IS TRUE, MR. BROWN, I ASK THE SAME QUESTIONS EACH YEAR ON THE FINAL HISTORY EXAMINATION. BUT, I ALWAYS CHANGE THE ANSWERS.

Enthusiasm cannot be taught. It is caught.

Behind each successful teacher is at least one student who knows how to operate the class computer and program the VCR.

Most reports show that a majority of teachers soon forget what they learned in the colleges of education.

The chief purpose for school credit unions is to help teachers live within their incomes.

During my first years as a classroom teacher, two qualities helped me to survive—good health and a poor appetite.

Some say insanity is hereditary. That is not always true. Some teachers catch it from their students.

"WHY NOT PLAY IT SAFE? GIVE HIM A D-"

I THINK IT'S ONLY FAIR TO WARN YOU, MISS BLACK. MY DAD SAID IF I DON'T PASS THE MATH TEST, THAT SOMEONE WAS GOING TO GET A GOOD LICKING.

It's a miscarriage of values when the school custodians are paid more than the teachers— unless they are worth it.

AND THEY HAVE A BETTER RETIREMENT SYSTEM, TOO.

I KNOW THE CUSTODIAN MAKES MORE MONEY THAN YOU DO, JOHN, BUT YOU CAN'T CHANGE PLACES WITH HIM.

Blessed are the students who constantly drive the teachers up a wall, for they shall soon become good friends of the school psychologist.

ABSENCE MAKES THE HEART GROW FONDER.

WHOM DID YOU BLAME THINGS ON WHILE I WAS ABSENT?

Designing a school curriculum can be compared to making chili. Often it's not what you put in the pot that makes it good, it's what you left out.

WHO NEEDS HEALTH BOOKS?

ARE YOU INTERESTED IN WHAT I LEARNED IN SCHOOL TODAY? MISS BROWN TOLD US ALL WE NEED TO KNOW ABOUT SEX.

Sex education is the course that takes the least amount of time to teach but often causes the most problems.

AT LEAST LET HIM TRY

HOW CAN YOU EXPLAIN SEX TO ME WHEN YOU DON'T UNDERSTAND THE NEW MATH.

The next time you see boys wearing rings in their noses and ears, keep in mind they will have removed them before they interview for their first jobs.

Teaching in a poverty-stricken school has one advantage. If you do something great, everyone who hears about it will be surprised. If you fail, few will care.

Superintendents do not suffer because they are misunderstood, but because they are understood.

When a teacher moves from the classroom to school administration, the intelligence level of both groups improves.

MAYBE HE GOT OUT BEFORE THE PETER PRINCIPLE CAUGHT UP WITH HIM.

YOU ASKED ME WHY I DIDN'T TAKE THE PRINCIPAL'S JOB WHEN IT WAS OFFERED TO ME. I'D RATHER HAVE YOU AND OTHERS WONDER WHY I DIDN'T TAKE IT THAN WHY I DID.

Some retired principals feel like overweight, retired football players: unfit to play football but good for nothing else.

OLD PRINCIPALS NEVER DIE. THEY JUST LOSE THEIR FACULTIES.

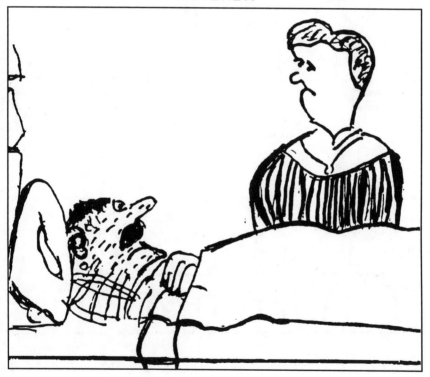

I DIDN'T KNOW PRINCIPALS GOT THE MEASLES.

The sports program in some schools is like a large friendly dog in a china shop. The more tail he wags, the more damage is done.

AND HE HAS TO PLEASE THE PARENTS, TOO.

WHAT DO YOU WANT — A WINNING FOOTBALL TEAM OR A GOOD EDUCATIONAL PROGRAM. WE CAN'T HAVE BOTH.

Appreciation is that happy day in the life of a teacher when a student says, "I enjoyed being in your class today."

Education authors are famous for writing books few will bother to read, hoping they can make enough money to pay for the ones they give away.

Blessed is the teacher who struggles through ice, snow, sleet and rain to get to school, only to discover classes have been canceled.

Educational writers don't repeat themselves, they merely repeat each other.

One sure way for a teacher to be praised—RETIRE!

Old coaches never die. They live to have one more losing season.

I DOUBT IF YOU WILL EVER HEAR THIS

IT DOESN'T MATTER WHETHER WE WIN OR LOSE. GO OUT AND HAVE FUN. BUT, IF WE DO WIN, PROMISE ME YOU WON'T CARRY ME OFF THE FLOOR ON YOUR SHOULDERS.

The more confused a school system becomes, the more employees needed.

Blessed are the superintendents who make no public statements, for they will not have to deny saying them.

NOT ALL CHILDREN ARE ANGELS

TO GIVE YOU AN IDEA OF WHAT A PROBLEM BRUCE IS, HIS MOTHER COMES TO THE PTA IN DISGUISE.

Thirty years is long enough to teach. If teachers haven't suffered enough misery in that time, they must be numb.

ROLL JORDAN ROLL

ARE YOU TELLING ME YOU HAVE A MASTER'S DEGREE IN EDUCATION AND YOU HAVE NEVER HEARD OF JORDAN?

Teachers must learn to fight for their principles. Or is it their principals?

Superintendents: When you have a weak levy campaign, you'd better have a sure-fire slogan.

One sure way to guarantee a new idea will not be considered is to turn it over to a committee.

Pessimism is when teachers believe all students hate them and discovery is when they realize they do.

Mark Twain said, "In the first place God made idiots. That was for practice. Then he made school boards."

I'VE DECIDED THERE IS NO WAY TO HANDLE THE SCHOOL BOARD. WHEN I DO SOMETHING RIGHT, THEY NEVER REMEMBER IT. IF I DO SOMETHING WRONG, THEY NEVER LET ME FORGET IT.

Some students learn quickly all the rules of a classroom teacher. How else would they know how to break them?

Educational experts believe all their theories to be factual and the facts they question to be theories.

Employees in the central office tend to make work for each other.

When a project is successful, the superintendent claims the credit. When it fails, someone else shoulders the blame.

The farther a person is from a school problem, the more idealistic are their solutions.

Affection is when a student brings a teacher a plate of brownies, and bravery is when the teacher eats them.

"EITHER THAT HISSING STOPS IN THIS CLASS OR I BLOW MY TOP."

If a little learning is a dangerous thing, how smart must a student be to be out of danger?

My off-the-cuff research showed that dull and boring teachers seldom had a good sense of humor.

If authors of history books didn't stretch the truth now and then, no one would ever bother to read them.

The reason the school year lasts longer for the ineffective teachers is because time drags when you hate what you are doing.

Every teacher plans for something, even to fail, at times.

STARTING THE TRIP ALL OVER AGAIN.

HONEY, I KNOW I AM 44 YEARS OLD AND HAVE
6 CHILDREN. I DON'T MIND BEING PREGNANT
AGAIN. IT'S THE THOUGHT OF THOSE PTA'S
AND PIANO RECITALS THAT UPSETS ME.

The PTA always meets on a teacher's bowling night.

WHAT CAN HE TELL THEM THE NEXT TIME?

MY FOLKS MISSED THE PTA MEETING LAST NIGHT.
I TOLD THEM IT WAS TONIGHT.

The opening yearly staff meeting is often so boring that teachers actually welcome the day when students finally arrive.

THERE WILL ALWAYS BE PRAYER AS LONG AS THERE ARE TESTS

"I'M HAVING AN ENGLISH TEST TOMORROW. I AM GOING HOME AND DIAL-A-PRAYER. DO YOU THINK IT WILL HELP?"

"WHY DON'T YOU TRY STUDYING INSTEAD?"

One way for English teachers to get students to read the assigned books is to tell them they have been banned by the school board.

When it comes to letters, it is more important that students learn how to write one than to earn one.

A special place in heaven will be reserved for substitute teachers.

One of the best definitions I've heard for an educational conference: "Hot air on a high level."

Gone are the days when the chief worry in a school was the occasional boy or girl smoking in the restrooms.

THEY DIDN'T READ THE SURGEON GENERAL'S REPORT.

THE GOOD NEWS IS, I KNOW WHERE THERE IS A GOOD
PLACE TO SMOKE IN THIS BUILDING. THE BAD NEWS IS
THE PRINCIPAL KNOWS WHERE IT IS, TOO.

NURSES DO MORE THAN LOOK FOR HEAD LICE.

MRS. ROBERTS, I DID NOT SAY WHERE YOUR SON
WOULD GO IF HE SMOKED. I MERELY SAID THAT
WHEREVER HE WENT, HE JUST MIGHT GET
THERE SOONER.

A reminder to teachers who complain about their principal being stupid: You could have his or her job if you were any smarter.

OLD PRINCIPALS NEVER DIE

BUT YOU HAVE TO GO TO SCHOOL. YOU ARE 43 YEARS OLD AND THE PRINCIPAL OF IT.

One-half of the teachers stated, in a survey, that they decided to teach because they wanted to do something in life other than just make money. The other half lied, too.

Teachers, be nice to your students. One of them may grow up and be your surgeon.

An age-old educational truth: Any new idea will be half as effective as an old, established one and will cost twice as much to administer.

Delusion is when the teacher believes the school board is going to grant a 10% salary increase.

English teachers are no different than other teachers—only more so.

IGNORANCE DOESN'T REIGN IN SOME CLASSROOMS, IT POURS.

"BOBBY, THIS IS ABOUT THE WORST COMPOSITION I HAVE EVER READ. I CAN'T BELIEVE YOU ALONE COULD MAKE SO MANY ERRORS."

"YOU'RE RIGHT, MISS BROWN! DAD HELPED ME WRITE IT."

Teachers have taken an important step to be successful when they are able to laugh at their mistakes.

Many educators probably have given serious thoughts to writing a book titled *Educational Band Wagons I Have Been On*.

All kindergarten teachers and cuddly dogs go to heaven.

Sooner or later, a student who gets into daily trouble and is never punished, will think everything he/she does is permissible.

Educational researchers are somewhat like people who go up blind alleys. They go up them to see if they are really blind.

Many students follow Mark Twain's advice and never allow schooling to interfere with their education.

WELL, AT LEAST SHE WAS CLOSE.

"MY DAD READ A REPORT TO MOM AND IT SAID THAT 79% OF AMERICANS ARE DEFICIENT IN MATH."

"WHY THAT'S ALMOST HALF!"

Too many state and national educational conferences are like severe electrical storms: lots of noise, everything lights up and suddenly everything turns dark again.

Some college libraries are storage rooms for thousands of educational books.

Two critical ages for school administrators are when they are too young and when they are too old.

HE'LL HAVE MORE TIME FOR GOLF, TOO.

"WHY ARE YOU RETIRING FROM TEACHING SO YOUNG? YOU ARE ONLY 55."

"IT'S LIKE THIS, I'D RATHER RETIRE ONE YEAR TOO SOON THAN BE CRITICIZED FOR RETIRING ONE YEAR TOO LATE."

Some health books are so racy that parents make their children carry them to school in brown paper bags.

Optimism is when the teacher believes the tuna casserole in the cafeteria is eatable.

Genius has a limit; stupidity seems to go on forever.

The golden age of education will always be what educators did 50 years ago.

Educational critics are people who never learned how to teach, but have written many texts telling others how.

Too many educators attempt to impart knowledge without first possessing it.

Principal's Law: The importance of the work justifies the stress it causes.

How some students describe a cafeteria: Run quick to. Eat quick at. Return quick from.

Blessed are the administrators who do not have the answers to the problems in education and know enough to keep their mouths shut.

The time is rapidly approaching when there won't be an individual alive who walked three miles to school.

When a principal arrives at school at 8 a.m. with six teachers on the sick list, he knows it will be at least a four-aspirin day.

ONLY HIS DOG LIKES HIM

*YOUR STUDENTS AT
CENTRAL MIDDLE SCHOOL AWAIT YOU.*

Always put off until tomorrow the solving of educational problems. By that time, the unsolved problem will have been replaced by a new one.

Lesson plans and the Bible have one thing in common. Both are revered and admired, but seldom read.

Education without intelligence is like owning a new car and trying to operate it without gasoline.

Good classroom substitutes are as rare as a grand slam in baseball.

Every school system has an allotted number of positions to be filled by mavericks and nonconformists.

You know you are an old-timer if you can remember when the four major problems in the schools were running in the halls, gum chewing, littering and turning around in a seat.

WHILE ON HIS KNEES, THE BOY WAS PRAYING —
FOR A NATURAL!

YOU SAY YOU WERE SHOOTING "CRAPS" WHEN I
CAUGHT YOU AND YOUR FRIENDS ON YOUR KNEES?
THANK GOODNESS! I THOUGHT YOU WERE PRAYING!

School superintendents know a mistake was made somewhere when the school treasurer reports a monetary surplus.

The most important problems facing some schools are parking for teachers, sex for students and athletics for parents.

Teachers never feel more miserable than on the days when the supervisor visits their classes and they discover that they left their grade books and lesson plans home on the kitchen table.

We keep telling teachers about the rewards of teaching, but they know the best reward is when they retire and are still sane.

Pragmatism is when a teacher finally realizes that some students will always be stupid.

"YOU SPELLED HYPOCRITE CORRECTLY. NOW USE IT IN A SENTENCE."

"IF I CAME TO SCHOOL WITH A SMILE ON MY FACE, I'D BE A HYPOCRITE."

Too much education is often more of a curse than too little.

The school superintendent is one of the few school employees who can be away from his/her office for two weeks without being missed.

Some educators never change. They know they will never skid if they remain in a rut.

Happiness as defined by most teachers: Snow days, small classes and no cafeteria duty.

Discovery is the day when the teacher realizes all students are not geniuses.

THE SO-CALLED "NEW MATH" IN THE SIXTIES AND SEVENTIES OFTEN BECAME "NO MATH."

WHAT DO YOU MEAN, DO I UNDERSTAND THE NEW MATH? I NEVER UNDERSTOOD THE OLD MATH.

For every solution of a school problem, two additional problems occur.

The most serious problem in education today is lethargy. But, as someone said, "So what! Who cares?"

Whoever said, "If it ain't broke, don't fix it" never taught.

Teachers, remember...you are an educator, not God.

The Professor of Education lied to you.

Educators who are thought to be lucky usually are lucky because of hard work and dedication.

Don't get excited when a school system makes announcements of drastic new programs. They are probably old ones with new names.

The pay increase that school personnel receive usually is barely enough to cover the additional taxes and extra retirement costs.

WHY NOT A BURGER KING WHOPPER?

WHAT DO YOU THINK OF OUR SALARY INCREASES? IF I'M LUCKY, I CAN BUY AN EXTRA "BIG MAC" EVERY MONTH.

Superintendents are considered to be effective leaders when they lead the community in the direction the community wants to go.

Tenure is a system that pays ineffective teachers the same salary as the talented ones.

Murphy's Law for Educational Hardware: When a piece of audio-visual equipment stops working, the spare part needed to repair it is the only one the coordinator does not have.

A guideline to follow to be a successful administrator: Walk at a fast pace when traveling between offices, keep your eyes focused straight ahead and always carry a clipboard with many papers attached to it.

Many Americans spend more money on pizzas and fast food than they do on education.

Getting inoculated with a small dose of education prevents many from catching the real thing.

I GOT 100 ON MY TEST TODAY,
60 IN HISTORY AND 40 IN SCIENCE.

Humility is when a teacher comes to school after appearing in traffic court for speeding.

You know you are an old-timer if you can remember when the teacher's association was not a union.

The amount of space needed to house the central office employees increases proportionally with the bureaucracy the central office creates.

Overheard in a restaurant: If it weren't for the crazy antics of our school board, we wouldn't have any entertainment in this town.

In many school systems, there are three ways to do things—the right way, the wrong way and the school board's way.

Some SCHOOL BOARDS are like a few CHURCH organizations. Singly they can do nothing, but together nothing can be done.

CARTER CITY SCHOOL BOARD

THE VOTE WAS 4 TO 1 IN FAVOR OF SENDING THE SUPERINTENDENT A GET-WELL CARD

Confusion is the week-long candy sale.

Ignorance and stupidity in some schools are like men's clothing—seldom out of style.

WHAT IS A GRADE? WHAT THE TEACHER SAYS IT IS.

WITH GRADES LIKE YOU HAD ON YOUR LAST REPORT CARD, YOU CERTAINLY CAN'T BE CHEATING!

Blessed are those students who hunger and thirst for a good education, for many will be disappointed.

WOULD YOU BELIEVE THIS? AFTER SPENDING FOUR YEARS IN PREP SCHOOL, GETTING READY FOR THE FIRST GRADE, I TOOK A TEST AND I FLUNKED OUT BEFORE I EVER GOT THERE!

Buddha says, "Believe nothing, no matter where you read it." If he were alive today he might say, "Reading educational books to improve one's teaching is about as effective as taking two aspirin tablets to cure the common cold."

WHY AREN'T YOU IN SCHOOL?

Too many high schools graduate 17-year olds with a 7th grade education.

The last books to be shipped when there is a curriculum change are the teachers' manuals. Corollary: If they are not shipped within six weeks, they were never printed.

Many taxpayers who vote on school levies all their lives never knowing what a mill is.

The seven last words of a mediocre teacher: "I never did it that way before."

90% of child prodigies are in the eyes of the beholder, a parent!

BE THANKFUL SHE DIDN'T HAVE TWINS.

I SPENT ONE HOUR WITH MRS. BROWN YESTERDAY AND SHE USED 55 MINUTES SHOWING ME PICTURES OF HER GENIUS SON.

To get a little R and R and to see old cronies are the two major reasons I attended educational conferences.

WELCOME HOME

WAIT UNTIL YOU HEAR WHAT HAPPENED WHILE YOU WERE AT THE PRINCIPAL'S CONFERENCE. WE HAD A BREAK-IN ON MONDAY NIGHT, ON TUESDAY SOMEONE STUFFED THE JOHNS WITH TOILET PAPER, ON WEDNESDAY SOMEONE SET OFF SOME FIRECRACKERS, ON THURSDAY. . . . .

A college degree and a teaching certificate define a person as a teacher, but it takes hard work and dedication to be one.

ACCORDING TO SOME TEACHERS, "DEDICATION DOESN'T PUT FOOD ON THE TABLE."

"WHY ARE YOU QUITTING TEACHING THIS YEAR?"

"I AM TIRED OF A JOB THAT BUILDS CHARACTER. I WANT ONE THAT PAYS REAL MONEY."

Too many of our public schools are becoming safe havens for delinquents rather than temples for those who have a desire to learn.

TAKE HIS COMPUTER PRIVILEGES AWAY FOR A DAY.

YOU NEED NOT PUNISH MY SON. PUNISH THE ONE NEXT TO HIM AND THAT WILL SCARE HIM.

Three gold star days in the life of a teacher: (1) The day summer vacation begins. (2) The day they retire. (3) The day they make that final payment to the credit union.

Wonderment is when a football coach looks into a mirror and says, "Oh, why can't I win at least one game?"

Have you ever noticed that the big boys playing the tuba in the school band tower over most members of the football team?

Those who oppose a school levy write more letters to the local newspaper editor than those who favor them.

Great teachers are blessed with two passions—a passion for what they teach and a passion for whom they teach.

Some suggestions on what to do with ungraded test papers: (1) Mail them to your congressman. (2) Start a paper drive. (3) Trade them with another teacher. (4) Toss them in the air. Throw away the ones that hit the floor. (5) Mail them to the postmaster in Detroit.

IT'S BACK TO THE SALT MINES.

ALL RIGHT, MR. SUPERINTENDENT, GO TO THE SCHOOL BOARD MEETING AND DO WHATEVER YOU DO.

Back of every successful principal is a faculty of excellent teachers.

Innocence is when a teacher volunteers to be a chaperone for an overnight school trip.

JUST BE THANKFUL, IT'S NOT AN OVERNIGHTER.

I VOLUNTEERED YOU TO BE A CHAPERONE TO TAKE OUR CLASS TO THE ZOO TOMORROW.

Good administrators are like jugglers. They always have at least three problems to worry about at the same time.

A major cause of teacher stress—a broken-down copy machine.

Blessed are those who have Ph.D.'s in education, for many are educated beyond their intelligence.

Students are divided into two classes—the dumb ones and the smart ones. And the smart ones do the dividing.

The chief cause of anxiety is anxiety.

Frustration is when a teacher loses all her grades and class records because of a computer malfunction.

Some teachers are underpaid as baby-sitters but overpaid as educators.

No teacher plans to fail, but a few fail to plan at times.

If you get an urge to overhaul the educational system, take a nap until the feeling goes away.

A teacher's strike and a divorce are somewhat alike. Parties of both sides hope for a quick settlement.

Old Coaches' Law: Too much practice makes pathetic.

Serendipity is when a teacher does something by accident that was superior to what was planned.

When new ideas in education don't work, it is probably because nothing can come from nothing. At the same time, any good workable idea will not go back to nothing.

A person with an education is like a billfold. The owner need not show those around him he has one.

Breaking an egg does not make an omelet. Neither does getting a teaching certificate make one a teacher.

Blessed are the teachers who expect no salary increases, for they shall not be disappointed.

Great educators do not make success a goal, it just happens.

Sometimes fortunes and educational ideas are similar; the more they glitter, the more suspicious of their values we should be.

Stuff—that material a principal secures for teachers because other teachers have it but won't use it after they get it.

In a properly run school system, the person sweeping the floors or serving the meals has as much dignity as the superintendent.

SCHOOL CUSTODIANS PLANNING THEIR DAY.

*THE TV IN ROOM 101 IS ON THE BLINK.
I GUESS WE'LL HAVE TO WATCH THE
FOOTBALL GAME IN ROOM 10.*

One of the surest ways to achieve academic notoriety is to write about something that much has already been written about and make it worse.

If a textbook is not liked by the teachers and students, the curriculum committee will seldom replace it.

Whoever said, "Things cannot get worse" never taught a class of 25 kindergartners with runny noses, dirty pants, crying for their mothers...

If a teacher does not gain control the first day of class, day two will be too late.

As school administrators move up the educational ladder with promotions and higher salaries, the less control they have over the programs.

Teaching can be compared to a person playing golf. The super teacher scores all birdies and pars, with an occasional eagle thrown in; the average teacher is content with pars and bogies; and the ineffective teacher's card is loaded with bogies and double bogies.

A teaching certificate and teaching credentials are nothing more than pieces of paper.

AND HE WON THE ANNUAL WALT DISNEY AWARD, TOO.

"WHO'S THE NEW TEACHER IN ROOM 106, YOU KNOW, THE ONE WITH THE BEARD?"

"HE'S NOT NEW. HE SHOWED SO MANY MOVIES, YOU PROBABLY HAVE NOT SEEN HIS FACE."

When a surgeon makes a mistake, one person suffers. When an ineffective teacher takes over a classroom of 25 children, they and their parents suffer.

The reason for superintendents not moving to other jobs is, once they move, all the past, present and future problems they leave behind will be blamed on them.

The best education is often provided by the schools who have the oldest buildings and the most outdated equipment.

The ideal of education hasn't changed much since Mark Hopkins referred to it as "a pupil on one end of a log and the teacher on the other."

Some college educators are like the Model-T's my grandfather drove: they all made the same noise.

The master teacher in physical education writes more in-depth lesson plans than "Throw out the ball."

He who laughs last probably missed being assigned to chaperone the seventh grade party.

Advice to beginning teachers: the first person you want to become good friends with is the school custodian.

Miserable teachers beget miserable teachers.

OUR LAST SUPERINTENDENT WAS KNOWN AS A "HIT AND RUN." HE STAYED IN OUR COMMUNITY JUST LONG ENOUGH TO GET THE PEOPLE MAD AND THEN HE MOVED ON.

After examining all the applications for the new superintendent, the school board will hire someone who did not apply for the position.

When a teacher shows slides to a class about his or her European trip taken the previous summer, one slide will always be in the projector backwards or upside down or both.

My beginning teachers were wiser than the experienced teachers—they took my advice.

The early bird gets the closest parking spot.

Teachers do not count on luck to survive. They depend on it.

IF YOU PROMISE NOT TO BELIEVE THE STORIES MARY BRINGS HOME FROM SCHOOL, I PROMISE NOT TO BELIEVE THE STORIES SHE CARRIES FROM HOME.

In public education, the good teachers are seldom adequately rewarded; neither are the mediocre ones.

Educator's theme song: "Everything Old Is New Again."

Too many high school curriculums are a mile long and two inches deep.

Some educational theories last about as long as a late spring snow.

Middle and junior high school students are like weeds—often their bodies grow faster than their minds.

Teachers cannot always manage time perfectly. There are days when the clocks run out before they do.

Money will not buy a good education, but it will pay the salaries of staff members to tell you why it won't.

School philosophies are usually updated every six or seven years or whenever the state inspection is held—whichever comes first.

Never be too critical of ineffective teachers. Without them, we would never appreciate the good ones.

Advice to teachers: When committee assignments are made, select the one with the most professional sounding name. It will seldom meet.

Does a superintendent understand what is going on if he or she brags about the superior educational program and the superior football team in the same speech?

Tough athletic training rules in some schools were written in order to have legitimate reasons to "slam dunk" third or fourth stringers off the team.

THE COACHES COUNT THE BALLOTS

I TOLD YOU BEFORE THE VOTING BEGAN THAT JIM WOULD BE THE CAPTAIN OF THE BASKETBALL TEAM.

The words of a veteran elementary principal continue to ring in my ears, when he said to me during my rookie year as a principal, "The topics we discussed in today's meeting will be the same ones you will be discussing when you retire." He was right!

Blessed is the teacher who helps select the new text in April and does not gripe about it in October.

One major difference between a football game and the learning game is the learning game never ends.

A veteran teacher of 30 years usually has spent the first ten years being an idealist, the second ten being a pragmatist and the final ten being a realist.

The months of June, July and August are, at best, only temporary cures for teacher stress and anxiety.

TRUTH IS STRANGER THAN FICTION.

FOR 35 YEARS I PRETENDED I LOVED TEACHING, AND DURING ALL THAT TIME, THE BOARD PRETENDED TO PAY ME.

The "key" formula in any school system is $P = DK$, where P equals prestige, D equals the doors to be opened and K equals the number of keys carried. This formula might help to explain why custodians have more prestige in a community than the superintendent.

All one has to do to be a teacher is accept a class of impossible students for 180 days without seeing a psychiatrist.

NEXT YEARS CLASS MAY BE WORSE.

YOU ASKED ME IF I BELIEVED IN MIRACLES. WITH THE CLASS I HAVE THIS YEAR, I RELY ON THEM.

Some superintendents have been called magicians, prophets, wise administrators, public relations experts, financial wizards, plus many other names not fit to print.

Retirement: That time in life when you are finally financially able to take that trip to Australia, but are too tired to do it.

A cold university classroom will get ten degrees warmer by scheduling an educational course there.   The "hot air" generated works wonders.

A teacher said before retiring,   "I'm tired of teaching." Later, she was heard to say,   "I'm tired of not teaching."

Curriculum is what goes on in a classroom after the teacher closes the door.

The three least credible ideas held by too many teachers are: (1) believing all students in their classes will be well-behaved, (2) believing everything they read in the educational journals and (3) believing the personnel in the central office have answers to all their problems.

Paraphrasing Lin Yutang, "There's nothing more beautiful than a healthy, wise old retired educator."

Cafeteria dilemma: When the school attendance is down due to inclement weather, the cafeteria will have a surplus of food. When the weather is good and attendance will be down, there will be a surplus of food. If the cafeteria happens to be short on food, school attendance will be nearly perfect.

TEACHERS NEED VITAMINS, TOO.

*DO YOU KNOW WHAT I SAW MISS BLACK DO TODAY?
I SAW HER SPIKE HER COFFEE WITH GERITOL.*

You can fool all the people some of the time, you can fool some of the people some of the time, but nobody can fool a good school secretary.

You know you are an old-timer if you can recall when schools began each day with the pledge to the flag.

Whoever said, "Taking something from one book and making it worse," must have been referring to educational authors.

Good superintendents are like ducks. Above the surface they appear unruffled. Below the surface they paddle like hell.

One has to be careful when quoting from books on education because if you quote them accurately it is plagiarism.

Formula to rate the educational efficiency of the school's central office: The number of secretaries multiplied by the words typed per minute. That product divided by the number of central office personnel equals EE. (Educational Efficiency).

No matter how thoroughly a teacher explains an item so no one will misunderstand it, at least five students will.

NOBODY'S PERFECT

"YOUR SON DIDN'T EVEN KNOW WHEN ABRAHAM LINCOLN DIED."

"HOW COULD HE? WE NEVER LET HIM READ THE OBITUARY COLUMN."

A hundred years ago Hester Pyrnne of *The Scarlet Letter* received an "A" for adultery. By today's standards her grade would be a low "C".

AT LEAST HE GOT AN "A" IN PHYSICAL EDUCATION

*DAD, WHAT DO YOU WANT ME TO DO?
STUDY HARD AND GET "A's" AND HAVE NO FUN,
OR GET "C's" AND ENJOY SCHOOL MORE?*

NEXT TIME YOU TAKE A TRUE-FALSE TEST, REMEMBER, WHEN YOU FLIP A COIN, HEADS IS ALWAYS TRUE AND TAILS IS FALSE. THAT'S WHY YOU FLUNKED.

OLD BALDY GAVE ME A "B" IN MATH. I SHOULD HAVE
HAD AN "A." HE DIDN'T LIKE MY BROTHER EITHER.

Blessed are purists in education, for no one understands
what they are talking about.

Superintendents face few new problems, only recycled old ones.

Most statistics in education are about as reliable and helpful as a bucket of warm spit.

Education is the only guarantee that freedom can forever be maintained.

You know you are an old-timer if you can remember when time-sharing meant togetherness and not computers, when a chip was a piece of wood and when hardware was found in hardware stores.

Another 90-10 law: 10% of the teachers cause 90% of the school's professional problems.

One of my teachers complained when I agreed to be her reference to secure a loan from the credit union, "Some people try to save the world and I can't save enough money to buy new tires for my car."

The teacher certification process keeps many talented people out of teaching.

True liberal education is when a school system allows a student to read the Bible, read *Playboy* and learn how to shoot pool.

Many administrators probably wonder why they moved from the classroom working a normal school year to become principals working 12 hours each day and 12 months each school year.

ISN'T HE SUPPOSED TO BE THE GIVER OF STRESS,
NOT THE RECEIVER?

HE'S THE HIGH SCHOOL PRINCIPAL. HE COMES IN
EVERY FRIDAY AND SITS THERE 'TIL EIGHT O'CLOCK
MUMBLING, "OH, WHY DID I EVER LEAVE THE
CLASSROOM FOR THIS?"

A good in-service program can be compared to shooting at a target with a rifle rather than a shotgun. The rifle zeros in on the target whereas the shotgun may miss the target altogether.

On the day when we had the biggest drug problem in the history of the school, I thought of the corollary to Murphy's Law, "When things appear to be getting better, you have overlooked something."

JOHNNY IS BOTH THE WORST AND BEST STUDENT IN MY CLASS. HE IS THE WORST BEHAVED AND HE HAS THE BEST ATTENDANCE.

The only resemblance between delinquency when I first began to teach and when I retired was that the word continued to be spelled with eleven letters.

The unexplainable law for the length of school board meetings says, "The fewer the items on the agenda, the longer the meeting."

While in college I had many theories on how to educate children. When I retired I discovered I had been educating children and with very few theories.

Don't knock mediocre teachers. They are always at their best.

I read once that if professional educators had titled the book, *Why Johnny Can't Read*, they could have chosen a much longer title, as: *Motivational Research on Johnny's Reading Disorders*.

A prized gobbledygook definition of spanking: practical negative reinforcement.

Many teachers never knew they had oversized classes until their unions told them.

The responsibilities of assistant football coaches varies. One told me that his only responsibility during a game was "to make sure the kicking tee was returned after an extra point or field goal try."

The operation of some public schools is becoming more and more like the operation of the federal government. Their budgets seldom balance, they often have new programs in need of funding and they employ too many people to run them.

3-2-1 law: Any new educational project will take three times as long as planned, will cost twice as much as budgeted and will work no better than the established one it was scheduled to replace.

The more of nothing school bureaucrats know about education the more lucrative are their assignments.

When young principals say stupid things, nobody hears them. When old principals say ill-natured things, everybody hears them.

The best advice I gave to teachers was, "Always do your best and a little more."

Some teachers spend their entire teaching career being failures and no one ever noticed it.

School superintendents who offer five-year plans to school boards usually have moved to another school before the plan is fully implemented.

A couple of my late-arriving teachers to meetings probably would agree with James J. Walker, who said, "If you get there before it's over you are on time."

When the superintendent tells the staff in November that the school year is going great, something has been overlooked.

I am not saying my initial teaching salary was small, but my paperboy always cashed my paycheck.

Never criticize a lazy teacher. According to some experts, laziness is the mother of nine out of ten inventions.

Murphy's Cafeteria Law: When the cafeteria cooks fail to make enough pizzas, the student ahead of you will get the last one.

I'M HERE TO COMPLAIN ABOUT THE CAFETERIA FOOD. IT IS NOTHING BUT SLOP, IT HAS NO TASTE AND JUST LOOKING AT IT MAKES ME SICK. THE COCKROACHES REFUSE TO EAT IT. AND, TO MAKE MATTERS WORSE, THEY GIVE YOU SUCH SMALL PORTIONS.

Too many students who have 100% attendance in schools bring their brains only 50% of the time.

I CHANGED MY GRADING STANDARDS THIS YEAR. IF ANY STUDENT SHOWS UP IN CLASS 50% OF THE TIME, I PASS HIM. I DON'T WANT HIM BACK.

Students have a right to sound education, but not an absolute right.

Good teachers are born, not made.

Some believe that the only job requirement of a good substitute is to keep the kids from tearing the building down.

Teachers who have "N" rules for the classroom will usually have "N plus 1" exceptions.

Some educational experts I knew were like narrow-necked bottles—the less in them the more noise they made pouring out.

Too many school curriculums can be compared to a smorgasbord—lots of quantity but short on quality.

"THIS FOOD TASTES FUNNY. IT TASTES LIKE LAST YEAR'S FOOD."

"THAT'S BECAUSE IT IS LAST YEAR'S FOOD."

You know you are an old-timer if you can remember when fast food was eaten during Lent and not served almost daily in the school cafeteria.

Sometimes, during my years as a school principal, I felt like the person who mounted a horse and rode off in all four directions at the same time.

111

The teaching tactics of some teachers can be compared to a man walking on his two hands. It is seldom done well.

The ineffective teacher with 20 years of experience fulfills the third part of the Ginsberg Theorem, "You can't even quit the game."

Teachers who are sixty years young are more effective than many teachers who are thirty years old.

The lack of an education is like a tree that has been cut down: neither can be easily replaced.

How many psychologists does it take to change a light bulb? No one will ever know because a test has never been written to check their ability.

WHO SAID THAT COUNSELORS DON'T EARN THEIR MONEY?

"HOW DO YOU MANAGE DAY AFTER DAY LISTENING TO STUDENT'S PROBLEMS AND STILL END THE DAY BEING SO COOL AND UNBOTHERED?"

"WHO LISTENS?"

Teachers who worried and fretted over the best method for teaching a unit often did something accidentally that was better.

Remember when students didn't need a calculator to multiply 9 x 8?

Three prerequisites to be a successful coach: (1) Good athletes. (2) Soft schedules. (3) Luck.

A majority of teachers know how to teach better than they do.

Remove all the quotes and undetected plagiarism from a majority of the education textbooks and you will be left with 25 pages of commas, periods and question marks.

A superintendent, explaining why he thought his salary was not too high, described his job this way, "A superintendent is like a bull. It's not the time he spends. It's the importance of what he does."

Two ways to make people aspire for an education is to ration it and make it as attractive as sin.

OR MAYBE AN ALIEN FROM OUTER SPACE STOLE IT!

HOMEWORK? I DON'T HAVE ANY. WOULD YOU BELIEVE MY DOG CHEWED UP MY COMPUTER DISK AND MY HOMEWORK WAS ON IT?

Schools can't give students brains and intelligence, so they give them diplomas.

All teachers need a little lubrication now and then.

Too many schools spend too much time entertaining the students and too little time educating them.

When Samuel Butler said, "For things said and never meant do oft prove true by accident," he may have been thinking of the many hidden messages that are so common in our daily conversations.

School buses arrive early at the bus stop when the students are late; they will arrive late when it is raining.

BETTER THAN SEEING A PSYCHIATRIST

THESE ARE THE SCHOOL BUS DRIVERS. THEY MEET HERE EVERY FRIDAY AT 4 P.M. AND DRINK UNTIL EIGHT TO CALM THEIR NERVES.

When the superintendent calls a principal and says, "Come to my office, I want to discuss a problem with you." This means: "I am lonely and need someone to talk to."

When a superintendent sends a subordinate a memo and the message reads, "Read, initial and return to me." This means: "If my plan doesn't work, I'll have someone to share the blame."

When the superintendent tells the public that athletics will be curtailed if the tax levy fails. This means: Absolutely nothing.

When the superintendent talks to the staff in September about the need for dedication. This means: "There is no money for salary increases."

I JUST HAD A CLOSE ENCOUNTER. . .OF THE THIRD GRADE!

GOOD TEACHERS

Come to school early to get the choicest parking places, and they remain around after school closes to impress others.

Are trained professionally, including an up-to-date real estate license in their permanent records.

Smile in the face of difficulty as though they have someone to blame it on.

Are the ones who have developed a method of losing all ungraded test papers.

Broaden their interests by always having a copy of the *National Enquirer* in their desk drawers.

See the good in others when they need someone to take their playground duty.

Are friendly with those who dislike the same people they dislike.

Do not return from two days of illness with a suntan.

Are sincerely concerned with every child, including the one who says, "Let's do something interesting for a change."

Can revel in another's success even though they got their masters from a correspondence school.

THE SEVEN STAGES OF A BEGINNING TEACHER

1. Stage of *anticipation* — The new teacher waiting for school to begin for the first time.

2. Stage of *diplomacy* — When the teacher meets parents at the first PTO meeting and tells them what a delight it is to have their child in class.

3. Stage of *bewilderment* — When the first grading period ends and the teacher has no idea what to write on the grade cards.

4. Stage of *realism* — When the teacher discovers all students are not geniuses.

5. Stage of *frustration* — When the teacher begins the second semester and discovers he or she is six weeks behind in all classes.

6. Stage of *accomplishment* — When the teacher makes it through the year without having to borrow money from the credit union.

7. Stage of *satisfaction* — When the teacher welcomes the first summer vacation with a feeling of accomplishment, and says, "I'll be back next year."

"FORGET MEDICINE, TEACHING, COMPUTERS, THE SCIENCES. . .THE BIG MONEY IS AND ALWAYS WILL BE **PLUMBING.**"

12 THINGS TEACHERS DID THAT PLEASED ME

When they volunteered for chaperoning.

When they did not gripe about the size of their classes.

When they participated in community activities.

When they gave individual help to students.

When they did not complain about the texts they were using.

When they had parental conferences.

When they attended school activities.

When they handled their own minor discipline problems.

When they quit smoking.

When they used the new material that was purchased for them.

When they did not abuse sick leave.

When they had positive things to say about others.

NOT 14,000 OR 1400,
BUT 14 THINGS THAT MAKE TEACHERS HAPPY

When *school* is closed for the day.

When *all students* in your class have an IQ of 125.

When you receive a *Master's Degree*.

When you finally learn how to use the *computer*.

When the *PTA* meeting has been canceled.

When a *student* says, "That sure is a great outfit you're wearing."

When the *week-long state evaluation* ends.

When the *counselor* is testing your classes.

When you find your *lost keys*.

When the *worst behaved student* in your class suddenly moves.

When your request for *two personal days* is granted.

When the *copy machine* is finally repaired.

When the *school board* agrees to a six percent salary increase.

When no *parent* calls to complain about grades.

"IT MAY LOOK OMINOUS...BUT EVER SINCE HAVING IT INSTALLED, CLASSROOM PRODUCTIVITY HAS BEEN UP 100%!"

THE ABC'S OF SUCCESS (OR FAILURE)

Mark Twain said this about success, "If at first you don't succeed, you are about average." Samuel Johnson said, "Advice is seldom welcome. Those who need it most, like it least."

Avoid bad habits. *Believe* in yourself.
Complete every assignment.
Do a little more than is required. *Enjoy* teaching.
Face each day with a smile.
Give it all you've got and a little more.
Hang on to those dreams. *Ignore* negative people.
Join in and help when you are needed.
Keep cool when things go wrong.
Listen with your ears and not your mouth.
Maintain a good sense of humor. *Never* lie.
Open your eyes to new ideas.
Please yourself and you will please others.
Quitters never win and winners never quit.
Read! Read! Read!
Share your talents with others.
Take control of your class on day one.
Use your time intelligently.
Visualize yourself being a successful teacher.
Work hard. *Want* to succeed.
Accelerate your efforts to be a super teacher.
You are your most important asset.
Zero in on your teaching goals.

"SHE'S THE MOST ENTHUSIASTIC TEACHER I'VE
EVER HAD."

THE EVALUATION PROCESS

People of all professions fall into four basic groups: (1) *Clever* (2) *Stupid* (3) *Lazy* and (4) *Industrious*. Most fall into two of the areas at the same time, seldom one and never three or four.

Here are six lessons in evaluating teachers I learned during my many years as a principal.

(1) If you give a difficult task to a lazy teacher, he/she will often find a way to solve it.

(2) Some incompetents develop a system to fool others.

(3) Competence always contains the seed of incompetence.

(4) It takes at least one person on a staff who is both lazy and stupid to appreciate the effective ones.

(5) Occasionally the best teacher on the staff will do some stupid things.

(6) Once in awhile I had a teacher who was both clever and stupid.

MORE HIDDEN MESSAGES

When the school secretary tells a parent, "The principal is in an important conference and I can't disturb him." This means: "He is talking to two boys who were caught smoking in the restroom."

When the school counselor tells a parent, "This particular test fails to show us anything significant to help in recommending a career possibility." This means: Your child is qualified to fill a position you own or have some influence in."

When a coach tells a parent "Your son has great potential." This means: "Your child has two left feet and is as clumsy as an ox."

When a teacher tells a parent, "Your child makes friends easily." This means: "Your child is the class clown."

**A SAMPLE OF THE ADVICE GIVEN TO EDUCATORS
FROM THE *"DEAR PAM COLUMN"*
IN THE DAILY NEWSPAPERS.**

To a Chicago principal: "If your school has serious educational problems with low test scores, high dropout rates and many students on drugs, my suggestion is 'Get yourself a better class of students'."

"IT'S VERY GENEROUS OF YOU, RUSSELL, BUT I DON'T BELIEVE YOUR RESIGNATION WOULD HELP OUR CROWDED SCHOOL SITUATION."

Advice to the Marion teacher who wanted to be sure she would not be accused of plagiarism when she published a book: "Do what many writers do. Steal from more than one source and make it worse." She then added a little humor by stating, "Remember all work and no plagiarism makes for a dull book."

Advice to the superintendent of Boise: "Remember, a good superintendent doesn't have to please everybody—just enough to keep the job."

Advice to Peoria's attendance officer on how to reduce truancy rates: "Lock the doors after school starts and turn a classroom into an arcade."

To the worried parent of Grover Hill who expressed concern over the rising number of high school dropouts: "Don't knock the problem. Having dropouts is the only way to guarantee some college graduates will get jobs."

To the counselor from Spaulding on the value of standardized tests: "I wouldn't give too many. They interfere with the student's natural ignorance."

OSCAR WILDE SAID, "IN EXAMINATIONS, THE FOOLISH ASK THE QUESTIONS THAT THE WISE CANNOT ANSWER."

I TOOK ONE OF THE APTITUDE TESTS WE GIVE TO THE STUDENTS AND I WAS TOLD TO DROP OUT OF SCHOOL AND TAKE UP A TRADE.

To the chairperson of the curriculum committee from Van Wert on the ideal size of a committee: "The size of a committee is unimportant because the real objective of a committee is not to reach a decision, but to avoid it."

To the beginning superintendent from Sidney who asked, "Is experience still the best teacher?" Her answer was: "Yes, I believe it is. How else would you be able to recognize your mistakes so you can repeat them?"

Advice to the school board member from the city of Reading: "Spend at least as much time for and hiring your new superintendent as you did your last football coach."

Advice to the principal in Charleston who asked Pam if she believed in gifted programs: "Not completely. Too many gifted programs are only ego builders for parents who have children in them."

A recently retired teacher from Kokomo wrote, "To stop using such terms as differential staffing, vertical articulation, homogeneous grouping."

TEACHERS - YOU KNOW IT'S GOING TO BE A BAD DAY WHEN -

The principal comes in for a visit and you have no lesson plans.

The counselor schedules a conference at 3:30 P.M.

The nurse can't find the medical records for your class.

The girl in the front row wets her pants.

Three new students arrive at school and you get two of them.

You arrive at school and you discover you have your pantyhose on backwards.

You open the classroom door and discover the custodian failed to sweep your room.

The custodian destroyed your coffee mug.

AND STILL MORE HIDDEN MESSAGES

When a teacher tells the class, "The answer to this math problem is obvious." This means: "I don't understand it either."

When a father tells a teacher, "My boy is so sensitive, you will have to handle him with kid gloves." This means: "My wife and I can't handle him at home either."

When a school psychologist tells a parent, "Your child is an underachiever." This means: "Your child is either stupid or just plain lazy."

When the football coach tells the Kiwanis Club, "I have a fine bunch of kids this year." This means: "Prepare for a losing season."

"I GOT ON THE SCHOOL BUS BY MISTAKE."

SURVIVAL KIT FOR TEACHERS
CONTENTS

A bottle of aspirin

The Bible

Application to borrow money from the credit union

A letter of resignation (Just in case)

A round-trip to Florida for the Christmas vacation

An extra pair of pantyhose just in case you don't quite make it

An extra bulb for the movie projector

A box of Kleenex

A bottle of Tums

A ten-dollar bill (Mad money)

A comprehensive insurance policy

An up-to-date Realtor's license

A bottle of multi-vitamins.

HIDDEN MESSAGES (Continued)

When the principal asks the superintendent a question and the answer is, "I'll give it some thought." This means: "I don't know the answer either."

When the principal asks the superintendent for some advice to a problem and hears, "See me in a week." This means: "By that time, you will have forgotten all about it."

THE FRACTURED SCHOOL YEAR

Average length of the school year
in the United States . . . . 180 days

Average time lost each day due
to school disruptions . . . . 30 minutes

TIME FOR THE MORNING ANNOUNCEMENTS

ALL TEACHERS AND STUDENTS —
WE WILL RUN SCHEDULE "A" THIS MORNING DURING THE TAKING OF SCHOOL PICTURES.

AT NOON WE WILL RUN THE REGULAR SCHEDULE EXCEPT THE LUNCH TIMES WILL BE REVERSED. SEVEN GRADE WILL EAT LAST, NOT FIRST.

THE AFTERNOON SCHEDULE WILL BE INTERRUPTED SO COUNSELORS MAY GIVE THE CALIFORNIA IQ TEST TO THE SEVENTH GRADES. OTHER SCHEDULE CHANGES WILL BE ANNOUNCED LATER.

SOME MAJOR SCHOOL DISRUPTIONS

Daily attendance taking.

Interruption by the school principal.

School sales (candy, magazines, etc).

Picture-taking days.

School delays due to bad weather.

Assemblies and other programs.

Students being called to the office.

Students upchucking.

Testing program by the school psychologists.

Camping and other outside programs.

30 minutes a day grows into 90 hours each year

or

The equivalent of three full weeks of school for class disruptions. This does not include students being absent, which averages 10% in some schools.

ALL I WANT FOR CHRISTMAS

Teacher: To have at least one student who knows how to use the computer and program the VCR in my classroom.

Student: To go two days without Miss Smith yelling at me.

Custodian: A compliment from at least two teachers for cleaning their rooms and washing their blackboards.

Principal: Two teachers to take hall duty during period V.

Superintendent: The passage of the two-mill levy to put new roofs on the school buildings.

Psychologist: To find two tests the teachers believe are worthwhile.

Football coach: Two running backs who can run faster than my grandmother.

Basketball coach: Two players who do not have two left feet.

Kindergarten teacher: Two fewer students in my class—and I get to choose them!

Bus driver: A bus that will run two days without breaking down.

Assistant principal: To be able to go two days without seeing Johnny Smith.

Counselor: To have two teachers who think I do more than give IQ tests to students.

School secretary: Mr. Egbert and Mrs. McDowell to have their attendance reports to the office on time two days in a row.

"AND JUST HOW LONG HAVE YOU BEEN DRIVING THE
SCHOOL BUS?"

THIS AND THAT

An industrial arts teacher of mine gave the son of a
complaining parent all "A's" for the remainder of the school
year in October, saying, as he handed the report card
back to the parent, "If you insist on your son having all
'A's', I'll give them to him now.

After my counselor finished describing the merits of a test he gave, he asked a group of parents, "Do you have any questions?" A woman in the front row broke the silence by asking, "Will you go back and explain everything you said after 'ladies and gentlemen'?"

On my last official day after the school's graduation assembly, a parent was quite unhappy with her son's report card of nearly all "F's". After she heard a number of parents wish me well on my retirement, she said, "I want to pay you the highest compliment. Thank heavens you are quitting."

I had a red face one day when I thought I was observing a teacher in a math class. After sitting for about 15 minutes, waiting for the class to start, the teacher finally noticed me. I hadn't realized I was observing a study hall.

A very pregnant teacher of mine assured me at 7:30 A.M. not to worry, saying, "I always deliver on time, never early." At 9 A.M. her husband picked her up, took her to the hospital and at 11 A.M., she was the mother of a baby girl. Moral: Never trust what a pregnant teacher tells you.

A superintendent, addressing a state meeting said, "I know I have to make some visible curriculum changes every five or six years. But I don't care what the curriculum says. Give me dedicated teachers and they can teach with ten-year old texts and still do a super job."

Every teacher should direct at least one play. After directing two for the experience, I directed three more for $100 a play. That figured out to be 13¢ an hour.

I tried to be democratic, just as my educational texts said I should do, during my early years as a principal. I soon learned that teachers expected me to make a majority of the decisions.

Sometimes I made statements to teachers off the top of my head that were more effective than the thought-out ones. My teachers often reminded me of an expression I made at a staff meeting, "Remember, a little ambiguity never hurt anyone. Learn to live with it."

During a staff meeting, I was discussing the need to tighten up on our discipline when a teacher offered this solution. "I know how to solve your problems," he said, "Let's have a public hanging every six weeks. That will tell the kids we really mean business."

"What do you mean you thought I would
bring the diplomas?"

The following school awards are ones I always wanted to give every spring but never had the nerve to do it.

NAME OF AWARD	RECIPIENT
ABSENCE MAKES THE HEART FONDER AWARD	Given to the teacher who missed the most school
PLAGIARISM AWARD	Given to the teacher who spent the most time at the copy machine.
BLAH-BLAH AWARD	Given to the teachers who received advanced degrees during the year
THE FASHION PLATE AWARD	Given to the sloppiest dressed teacher in the building
THE PUNCTUALITY AWARD	Given to the teacher who was the most often late to meetings.
THE EASTMAN KODAK AWARD	Given to the teacher who showed the most movies.
SILVER STAR AWARD	Given to all teachers who taught for thirty years and were still sane.

GETTING THAT LAST KID READY AND OFF TO SCHOOL

Also Available from Lincoln-Herndon Press:

*Grandpa's Rib-Ticklers and Knee-Slappers	$ 8.95
* Josh Billings—America's Phunniest Phellow	$ 7.95
Davy Crockett-Legendary Frontier Hero	$ 7.95
Cowboy Life on the Sidetrack	$ 7.95
A Treasury of Science Jokes	$ 9.95
The Great American Liar—Tall Tales	$ 9.95
The Cowboy Humor of A.H. Lewis	$ 9.95
The Fat Mascot—22 Funny Baseball Stories and More	$ 7.95
A Treasury of Farm and Ranch Humor	$10.95
Mr. Dooley—We Need Him Now!	$ 8.95
A Treasury of Military Humor	$10.95
Here's Charley Weaver, Mamma and Mt. Idy	$ 9.95
A Treasury of Hunting and Fishing Humor	$10.95
A Treasury of Senior Humor	$10.95
A Treasury of Medical Humor	$10.95
A Treasury of Husband and Wife Humor	$10.95
A Treasury of Religious Humor	$10.95
A Treasury of Farm Women's Humor	$12.95
A Treasury of Office Humor	$10.95
A Treasury of Cocktail Humor	$10.95
A Treasury of Business Humor	$12.95
A Treasury of Mom, Pop & Kid's Humor	$12.95
The Humorous Musings of a School Principal	$12.95
A Treasury of Police Humor	$12.95
A Treasury of Veterinary Humor	$12.95

*Available in hardback

The humor in these books will delight you, brighten your conversation, make your life more fun, and healthier, because "Laughter is the Best Medicine."

Order From:
Lincoln-Herndon Press, Inc.
818 South Dirksen Parkway
Springfield, IL 62703
(217) 522-2732
FAX (217)544-8738